PHILLIS
WHEATLEY
SLAVE AND POET

SPECIAL LIVES IN HISTORY THAT BECOME

Signature LIVES

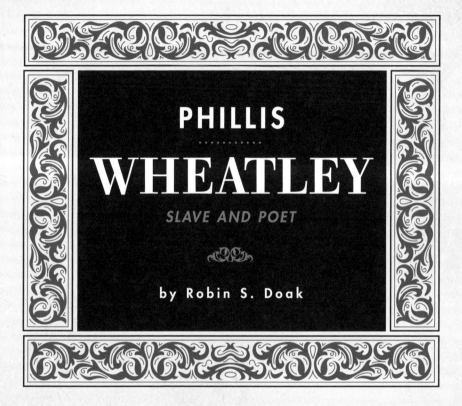

PHILLIS
WHEATLEY
SLAVE AND POET

by Robin S. Doak

Content Adviser: Pamela R. Fletcher,
Assistant Professor of English,
The College of St. Catherine

Reading Adviser: Rosemary G. Palmer, Ph.D.,
Department of Literacy, College of Education,
Boise State University

COMPASS POINT BOOKS ✦ MINNEAPOLIS, MINNESOTA

Compass Point Books
3109 West 50th Street, #115
Minneapolis, MN 55410

Visit Compass Point Books on the Internet at *www.compasspointbooks.com*
or e-mail your request to *custserv@compasspointbooks.com*

Editor: Sue Vander Hook
Lead Designer: Jaime Martens
Page Production: Noumenon Creative
Photo Researcher: Svetlana Zhurkin
Cartographer: XNR Productions, Inc.
Educational Consultant: Diane Smolinski

Managing Editor: Catherine Neitge
Creative Director: Keith Griffin
Editorial Director: Carol Jones

Library of Congress Cataloging-in-Publication Data
Doak, Robin S.
  Phillis Wheatley / by Robin S. Doak
    p. cm. — (Signature lives)
  Includes bibliographical references and index.

  ISBN 0-7565-0984-X (hardcover)
  1. Wheatley, Phillis, 1753-1784—Juvenile literature. 2. Poets,
American—Colonial period, ca.1600-1775—Biography—Juvenile literature. 3. Slaves—United States—Biography—Juvenile literature. 4. African
American poets—Biography—Juvenile literature. I. Title. II. Series
PS866, W5Z845 2006
811'.1—dc22   2005002708

REVOLUTIONARY WAR ERA

The American Revolution created heroes, and traitors, who shaped the birth of a new nation—the United States of America. "Taxation without representation" was a serious problem for the American colonies during the mid-1700s. Great Britain imposed harsh taxes and refused to give the colonists a voice in their own government. The colonists rebelled and declared their independence from Britain— the war was on.

PHILLIS WHEATLEY

BORN IN WEST AFRICA AND SOLD AS A SLAVE FROM THE SHIP *PHILLIS* IN COLONIAL BOSTON

Phillis Wheatley

Table of Contents

1 OCEAN VOYAGE

❧◦❧

The small, thin girl trembled and shook in the hot summer sun. Wearing only a dirty piece of old carpet, the hungry, ill child huddled close to the others who had been shipped to this strange land. These newest Africans to arrive in North America in 1761 looked at their surroundings and wondered why crowds of white men and women were looking them over so carefully. Why were they here? What would happen to them now?

The ocean voyage from Africa to Boston, Massachusetts, had been long and hard. Thoughts of the horrible months on the ship were probably still on the minds of these kidnapped people. The little girl had somehow survived the long, dreadful trip, but many others had not been so fortunate.

Africans were brought to North America as early as 1619 on a Dutch slave ship.

The living conditions onboard the *Phillis* had taken many lives. Filth, stench, disease, and death had been in every part of the ship, especially in the hold below the deck. Hundreds of Africans were packed into that seafaring prison in spaces much too small for so many people. In order to squeeze more in, the crew forced them to lay side-by-side on wooden bunks. The head of one African touched the toes of another.

All day and night they were chained in that position. Occasionally, they were allowed to go on deck for short times of exercise. But some Africans chose that time to end their suffering by jumping into the sea to die.

The little girl probably stayed in a separate hold for children and women, who were often physically abused by the ship's crew. Once or twice a day, she ate gruel, a sort of watered-down oatmeal. Sometimes she may have eaten small bits of fish, rice, yams, or beans.

It was nearly impossible to stay well on slave ships. Diseases like dysentery, smallpox, and measles spread quickly. Often, the holds were covered in vomit, blood, and other body fluids. The smell was overwhelming. One of every four Africans usually died before arriving in North America. Their bodies were often dumped into the sea. On one voyage, 109 of the 167 Africans died before they reached

Captured Africans crowd onto the deck of a slave ship.

the American colonies.

But somehow, this little girl was still alive. On July 11, 1761, her ship sailed into the port at Boston. John Avery, the slave trader, would take over from there. He had spent months connecting with people in Africa to buy slaves and trade goods for others. Most of them were from places like Senegal, Sierra Leone, and islands off the coast of Guinea. Now that they had arrived, it was Avery's job to sell every African for the highest price on the auction block.

When the captain of the ship handed over the girl and the rest of the sickly group, Avery may have been doubtful about how much money he could make off this shipload of slaves. He may have wondered about the small African girl, who was described as just "a slender frail, female child, supposed to have been about seven years old, at this time, ... shedding her front teeth." Still, Avery advertised the sale in the *Boston Evening Post* and the *Boston Gazette and Country Journal.* The newspaper ad read:

> *A Parcel of likely Negroes, imported from Africa, cheap for cash, or short credit; ... Also, if any Persons have any Negro Men, strong and hearty, tho' not of the best moral character, which are proper Subjects for Transportation, may have an Exchange for small Negroes.*

Within a couple of weeks, the slave dealer was ready for the auction. The African girl stood there in the heat, not knowing what was about to happen to her. But she really didn't know what it meant to be purchased or to be a slave. The life she was about to begin as a slave was something she knew nothing about.

She also didn't realize that she possessed a wonderful talent that would one day make her famous.

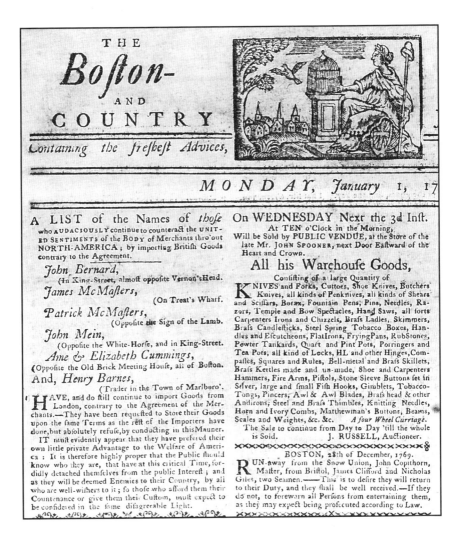

Her ability to write beautiful poetry would cause important people to notice her. Her poems would allow her to visit with some of the Founding Fathers of the United States of America. Who would have known that this little slave girl one day would also be invited to visit with a king?

2 OUT OF AFRICA

❧❀❧

The slave auction in late July 1761 was attended by many people. Bostonians were interested in the sale of the Africans who had arrived on the *Phillis*. John Wheatley was there that day. This very rich merchant and landowner owned a warehouse, a wharf, and a large sailboat called the *London Packet*. Now he wanted to buy a slave. His wife, Susanna, was getting older and needed someone to tend to her needs. Her slaves were also getting old, and Susanna wanted someone young enough to care for her and be her companion for the rest of her life.

There were many slaves to choose from. The Wheatleys thought about bidding on several strong, healthy-looking females. But something about the skinny little African girl with the large, sad eyes

An auctioneer sells an African slave to the highest bidder at a slave auction.

appealed to Susanna. John Wheatley purchased her "for a trifle," as a member of the family remembered. She went for a very low price, since "the captain had fears of her dropping off his hands ... by death." The Wheatleys got what they came for. They bundled the young child into their carriage and headed for home.

The little slave girl needed a name. Although she probably had an African name, she couldn't tell the Wheatleys what it was. She couldn't speak English, so she couldn't introduce herself and explain who she really was. It was impossible for her to describe where she was born in 1753—or maybe it was 1754. Memories of her mother and the rest of her family would stay hidden in her mind. She couldn't talk about the friends she left behind. Perhaps by now, they also had been taken and sold as slaves.

Slave traders had been capturing people in Africa long before this little girl was snatched from her home. As early as the 1600s, the west coast of Africa was a center for slave trade. African tribes would capture members of enemy tribes and sell them to European and American slave traders. By the 1700s, as many as 3,500 people were sold and shipped out of Africa each year. The slave trade provided a lot of money for many Africans, and it became an important part of West Africa's economy. For Americans, it provided free labor. Slaves worked their entire lives without being paid.

The Wheatleys' new little slave couldn't describe her capture or her horrible trip across the ocean. But another slave, Olaudah Equiano, told what it was like to be kidnapped. He wrote about how he was captured in Nigeria when he was 11 years old:

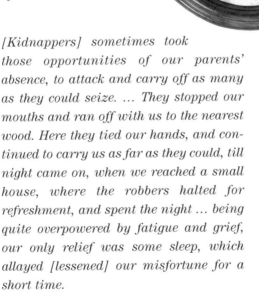

> *[Kidnappers] sometimes took those opportunities of our parents' absence, to attack and carry off as many as they could seize. ... They stopped our mouths and ran off with us to the nearest wood. Here they tied our hands, and continued to carry us as far as they could, till night came on, when we reached a small house, where the robbers halted for refreshment, and spent the night ... being quite overpowered by fatigue and grief, our only relief was some sleep, which allayed [lessened] our misfortune for a short time.*

Olaudah Equiano (1745?-1797) was an African slave and writer.

Kidnapped Africans were taken to slave forts, which were large stone buildings that served as prisons. There they waited in tiny, dark rooms with no beds. Some slaves stayed outside in pens like animals. Food and drink were scarce, but they only had to stay alive until the next slaving ship arrived. Then their captors herded them down to the shore and rowed them out to the ship.

The slave forts may have been terrible, but the worst was yet to come. Olaudah and the little girl both experienced it—the horrific sea voyage that took them out of Africa.

Captured Africans wait to be shipped to another country and sold into slavery.

The young girl would never talk about her voyage, her African name, or her life in Africa, even after she learned English. She was starting a new life with a new name—Phillis, after the name of the ship that brought her to North America. Her full name was

Phillis Wheatley, since slaves took on their owners' last names.

The carriage ride took Phillis through Boston, the capital city of Massachusetts. Boston was a chief port, where ships imported and exported goods daily. It was a center of trade and industry. More than 15,000 people lived there, and nearly 1,000 of them were black slaves. Just a few black people lived there as free citizens.

> *The first slave ship directly from Africa arrived in the American colonies in 1655. The Africans were sold at a slave auction in New Amsterdam, which was later renamed the colony of New York.*

Finally, Phillis got her first look at her new home. There on the corner of King Street and Mackerel Lane was the Wheatley house, one of the finest in the city. King Street was the busiest road in Boston. Its many houses and shops made it the heart of Boston's social and business worlds. Just a few blocks from the Wheatley house was the Old Colony House, where government officials met to make decisions for the Massachusetts Bay Colony.

Phillis was living in an important city with a very well respected family. She was one of the luckier slaves; her owners were very kind. Susanna had chores for Phillis to do, but she also wanted to educate her and encourage her to learn. She hoped her little slave girl would be her friend and companion as well.

3 LITTLE SLAVE

❦

Phillis Wheatley suited her new owners perfectly. Even the Wheatley children, 18-year-old twins Mary and Nathaniel, liked this quiet, shy, well-mannered slave. The family was good to Phillis, making sure she was well fed and properly clothed.

It wasn't long before the Wheatleys noticed something special about Phillis. She was intelligent, curious, and quick to learn. She saw how others were writing with a pen, and she tried it herself. The Wheatleys found letters and figures of all kinds that she had written on the walls with a piece of chalk or charcoal.

With her parents' permission, Mary began teaching Phillis to write. She also taught her how to read the Bible. Teaching a slave to read and write at this time was very unusual. In some colonies, it was

A young slave serves guests at a plantation home.

against the law to teach slaves these skills. Many believed knowledge might make slaves rebellious and more likely to disobey and run away.

John Wheatley noticed Phillis' amazing progress. He remembered later how much she had learned in her first 16 months at their home:

> *Without any Assistance from School Education, and by only what she was taught in the Family, she, in sixteen Months Time from her Arrival, attained the English Language, to which she was an utter Stranger before.*

Cotton Mather (1663-1728), pastor of the Congregational Church in Boston

Phillis lost herself in learning. Once she mastered reading, she began to study all kinds of poetry, from classical to modern. She studied geography and history and even learned French, Latin, and Greek. Guests of the Wheatleys were amazed at her quick grasp of these subjects. Visitors often encouraged her love of reading and writing by lending or giving her books. One of those people was Mather Byles, minister of the Congregational Church in Boston. In the early days of the American colonies, he joined his father as one of the ministers of the Second Church in Boston. Byles not only preached on Sundays, but he also wrote poetry.

Byles had a famous uncle—Cotton Mather, the respected minister of Boston's Old North Church in the late 1600s. When Mather died, Byles inherited his collection of books. He allowed Phillis to look through his library and read any of his books. He probably showed her the works of Alexander Pope, the English poet that became her favorite. Byles often wrote letters to Pope in England.

Samson Occom (1723-1792), American Mohican Indian preacher, missionary, and hymn writer

Another visitor to the Wheatley household was the Reverend Samson Occom, an American Mohican Indian who converted to Christianity and became a minister. Phillis wrote one of her first letters to him when he left the colonies to visit England in 1765. She was only about 12 years old when she began writing letters to many

> _Cotton Mather (1663-1728) was a leading religious leader in the Massachusetts Colony. He wrote about 450 published works, most of them sermons about how to know and serve God. Mather preached that individuals must have a personal experience with God to be saved. One of his most famous works is_ Magnalia Christi Americana, _a history of Christianity in New England in the 1600s._

people. Some of them were to the famous people she met at the Wheatley home, and others were to friends, especially her friend and fellow slave, Obour Tanner.

Phillis and Obour might have been together on the ship from Africa. Obour was also purchased by a kind family and given the opportunity to learn and develop her abilities. These two slaves could both read and write, which was an unusual situation in those times. They kept in touch through letters and remained friends throughout their lives. Phillis may have even visited Obour at her home in Newport, Rhode Island.

By her early teens, Phillis had an education that was better than what most upper-class young people in Boston had at the time. It was not considered important for girls to go to school then. Most young women just learned how to cook and run a household. So it caused quite a stir in Boston when Phillis, at the age of 14, translated a Latin poem into English. The poem, written by a Roman poet named Ovid, was about Niobe, a Greek queen who grieved endlessly for her dead sons and daughters.

Phillis Wheatley hoped to publish this hand-written poem, "To the University of Cambridge," written in 1767 at the age of 14.

The gods eventually turned Niobe into a rock that spouted water.

It was remarkable that a young woman would be

educated enough to know Latin. But it was very unusual that an African slave would be educated at all. She amazed many people, and they wondered why she was so different from the rest of the slaves in their community. Susanna Wheatley recognized how special she was, too, and kept Phillis separated from the rest of the slaves. Phillis wasn't allowed to socialize with the cook, the coachman, or the older slaves. She ate at her own table, separate from the Wheatleys and apart from the other servants.

Phillis no doubt felt lonely and strange. She was

A slave fans dinner guests to keep them cool in the heat of summer.

treated well, but she didn't feel part of the Wheatley family or part of the group of slaves. She didn't fit in anywhere. The Wheatleys made sure that Phillis never forgot she was different. Once, Susanna Wheatley sent the family carriage to pick up Phillis at another home. Susanna was horrified to find Phillis riding up front with Prince, the coachman. It was told that Susanna said, "Do but look at the saucy [daring] valet, if he hasn't the impudence [disrespect] to sit upon the same seat as my Phillis."

Susanna Wheatley's slave had become very important to her. Once in a while, she asked Phillis to do light housekeeping chores, but mostly she encouraged her to learn. Her intelligence gave her privileges that were unheard of for most slaves in the colonies. If Phillis felt like reading a book or writing a poem, the Wheatleys encouraged her to put her chores aside.

Phillis had her own bedroom with a candle and writing materials. Her room was heated, which also was unusual for a slave's quarters. If she got any poetic ideas during the night, she could get up, light the candle, and write them down.

John Wheatley remembered that his young slave began to write poetry when she was about 11 or 12. As she wrote more and more poems, Susanna Wheatley tried to get people to notice them. She wrote letters and invited well-known people to their home to read the girl's poetry. She submitted one of the poems to the *Newport Mercury*, a newspaper in Newport, Rhode Island.

On December 21, 1767, Phillis' poem, "On Messrs. Hussey and Coffin," appeared in the newspaper. It was the first time any of Phillis' works was printed. The poem was dedicated to two men who had once visited the Wheatley household. She knew them just as Mr. Hussey and Mr. Coffin. During their stay, they told the Wheatleys of their terrifying tale of narrowly escaping drowning during a storm at sea. Phillis wrote down their ordeal in verse. The poem also showed how strong Phillis' religious faith was. She wrote:

> *Suppose the groundless Gulph had snatch'd away*
> *Hussey and Coffin to the raging Sea;*
> *Where wou'd they go? where wou'd be their Abode?*
> *With the supreme and independent God,*
> *Or made their Beds down in the Shades below.*

Phillis Wheatley was often ill, and that gave Susanna one more reason to give her special treatment. Phillis was weak and fragile when she arrived in Boston, and she continued to get sick regularly. She suffered from asthma, making it difficult for her to breathe. She may have had tuberculosis, a disease that affects the lungs. The Wheatleys made sure she got constant medical attention.

Phillis became so ill one year that Susanna sent her away to recover. Phillis wrote to her friend Obour:

> *I have been in a very poor state of health all the past winter and Spring, and now reside in the country for the benefit of its more wholesome air.*

Phillis' health improved, and she returned to Boston and to her life as a slave. Despite her special

Boston in the mid-1700s

privileges, she was still a slave. The Wheatleys controlled her life and her future. They were gentle and kind, but kindness was not a substitute for freedom. Phillis had little hope for life as a free woman.

Her poems were about many subjects and people, but she usually didn't write down her feelings on slavery. However, part of her poem, "To the Right Honourable William, Earl of Dartmouth," described how she felt:

> Should you, my lord, while you peruse my song,
> Wonder from whence my love of Freedom sprung,
> Whence flow these wishes for the common good,
> By feeling hearts alone best understood,
> I, young in life, by seeming cruel fate
> Was snatch'd from Afric's fancy'd happy seat:
> What pangs excruciating must molest,
> What sorrows labour in my parent's breast?
> Steel'd was that soul and by no misery mov'd
> That from a father seiz'd his babe belov'd:
> Such, such my case. And can I then but pray
> Others may never feel tyrannic sway?

Phillis Wheatley remembered Africa, and she remembered the dreadful day when she was taken from her home and family. Although she never talked about her mother and father or any other relatives, she recalled in poetry how painful it was for them when she was taken away. Wheatley's deep sorrow over her past sparked within her a desire for

Village in the valley of the Congo River, Africa

freedom. She longed for her personal freedom, but she also hoped that all other slaves would one day be free. ✑

Chapter
4 AN UNUSUAL GIRL

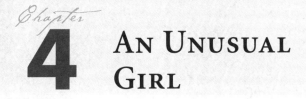

Poetry became more and more important to Phillis Wheatley. She studied the works of other poets and continued to write her own poetry. Her favorite poets were African writers, and some-times she wrote poems about them. One was about Terence, a black Roman writer who lived in the second century B.C. Perhaps she felt a connection to this African who was brought to Rome, Italy, as a slave and educated by his master. One day, Terence's master set him free. Phillis could only hope that might happen to her.

Religion grew to be more significant in Phillis' life. She found that writing poems was the perfect way to combine her love of learning with her faith. She included references to the Bible and

Phillis Wheatley attended church services at the Old South Church in Boston, Massachusetts.

Greek mythology in many of her poems. At the age of 14, she wrote "On Being Brought From Africa to America," a poem of gratitude for being brought to the colonies where she could understand about God. She wrote of the "mercy" of being enslaved in order to become a Christian. She reminded Christians that blacks, too, can come to God.

> *'Twas mercy brought me from my Pagan land,*
> *Taught my benighted soul to understand*
> *That there's a God, that there's a Saviour too:*
> *Once I redemption neither sought nor knew.*
> *Some view our sable race with scornful eye,*
> *'Their coulour is a diabolic die,'*
> *Remember, Christians, Negroes, black as Cain,*
> *May be refin'd, and join th'angelic train.*

The Wheatleys regularly attended the New South Church in Boston. But Phillis chose instead to attend the Old South Church. Like other black people, she had to sit in the balcony during services, away from white churchgoers. In 1771, Phillis was baptized at her church. That same year, Mary Wheatley married John Lathrop, the minister of another Boston church, the Old North Church.

Phillis was an active church member. She took her faith very seriously and told how it gave her life meaning and purpose. Her life was not just filled with poetry and religion, however. She hardly could

Inside the Old South Church in Boston, Massachusetts

avoid the political conflicts going on around her.

Since 1765, just four years after she arrived in Boston, people had been upset about the way the British were ruling the colonies. There had even been rioting in the streets of Boston. In 1765, Britain had passed the Stamp Act, requiring citizens of all the colonies to buy a stamp for almost everything written or printed on paper. Newspapers, wills, deeds, and even playing cards had to be stamped. The colonists were outraged. They felt the British had no right to make them pay this tax. After all, they had no one representing them or speaking for them in the British Parliament. Angry mobs took to the streets of Boston. They stole from the homes of British officials and threatened anyone who supported the new tax.

Some of the more violent protesters beat up tax collectors and chased them out of the Massachusetts Colony. Others tried peaceful ways to protest and decided to talk directly to British lawmakers. One of those people was Benjamin Franklin. He helped form the Stamp Act Congress, which encouraged colonists not to pay the stamp tax. Finally, the British Parliament made the decision to repeal the Stamp Act. For a while, the colonists were satisfied.

But by 1770, Britain passed more tax laws and sent more soldiers to the colonies. Bostonians were angry that the red-uniformed British troops were in their city. Sometimes, they threw rocks at them and called them names like redcoats and bloodybacks. Fights broke out more and more often. The worst clash happened on March 5, 1770. Colonists were throwing rocks and insulting a group of redcoats, when the British opened fire. Three colonists were killed, and two died later.

This fight, which came to be called the Boston Massacre, took place just down the street from the Wheatley house. Phillis was deeply affected by it

Angry colonists and British soldiers fight outside the State House in Boston, Massachusetts, in what came to be called the Boston Massacre.

and put her feelings into poetry. Her poem, "On the Affray in King Street, on the Evening of the 5th of March, 1770," appeared in the *Boston Evening Post*. Although her name was not on the poem, people who knew her recognized it as her work. The short poem honored four of the fallen colonists. One of them, Crispus Attucks, was a black man.

Long as in Freedom's Cause the wise contend,
Dear to your unity shall Fame extend;
While to the World, the letter's Stone shall tell,
How Caldwell, Attucks, Gray, and Mav'rick fell.

Preacher and evangelist George Whitefield (1714-1770).

That same year, on September 30, the famous English evangelist and preacher George Whitefield died. Phillis was deeply moved by his death. He was in Boston just the month before, preaching outdoors in his booming voice to thousands of people. He preached to huge crowds on the streets of Boston, and Phillis most likely went to hear him. His message agreed with Phillis' strong religious beliefs. She put her feelings into an elegy, a poem expressing sorrow for a person who has died.

Elegies were popular in the colonies. People believed they gave comfort to the family and friends of the person who died. Phillis called her 62-line elegy "An Elegiac Poem, on the Death of that Celebrated Divine, and Eminent Servant of Jesus Christ, the Late Reverend, and Pious George Whitefield." The first part praises the great preacher:

Hail, happy saint, on thine immortal throne,
Possest of glory, life, and bliss unknown;
We hear no more the music of thy tongue,
Thy wonted auditories cease to throng.

Thousands of people came to hear George Whitefield preach on his tours in England and America.

Thy sermons in unequall'd accents flow'd,
And ev'ry bosom with devotion glow'd;
Thou didst in strains of eloquence refin'd
The Greatest gift that ev'n a God can give,
He freely offer'd to the num'rous throng,
That on his lips with list'ning pleasure hung.

Phillis Wheatley wrote many elegies; one was "On the Death of Dr. Samuel Marshall."

The elegy was signed—"By Phillis, a servant girl of 17 years of age, belonging to Mr. J. Wheatley, of Boston:—And has been but 9 years in this country from Africa."

The elegy for Whitefield got a lot of attention. *The Massachusetts Spy* newspaper published it first. Then it was reprinted as a broadside, a large sheet of paper printed on one or two sides. The broadside was distributed as a pamphlet throughout Boston. Later, the poem was printed in newspapers in New York City; Newport, Rhode Island; and Philadelphia, Pennsylvania. In 1771, it was printed in London, England.

The elegy was making Phillis Wheatley famous. The Wheatley home hummed with activity as people began dropping by to see this unusual black slave girl who could write beautiful poetry. Thomas Woolbridge, a friend of George Whitefield, stopped by the Wheatley house on his way through Boston. He wanted to meet this amazing slave-poet who

George Whitefield (1714–1770), minister of the Church of England, traveled between England and the American colonies in the mid-1700s, preaching about 10 times a week. Large crowds of several thousand came to hear him. When buildings could not hold the crowd, Whitefield took his meetings outside. At one revival, 100,000 people gathered to hear this man whose voice, it was said, could be heard for a mile. The rich and poor, the famous and unknown responded to his message of salvation. Jonathan Edwards and John Wesley also preached in England and America. Together, these evangelists were responsible for changing the religious and social life of two nations. The movement came to be known as the Great Awakening.

had written such a beautiful poem about his friend. Woolbridge later wrote:

> *While in Boston, I heard of a very Extraordinary female Slave, who made some verses on our mutually dear deceased Friend [Whitefield]; I visited her mistress, and found by conversing with the African, that she was no Imposter; I asked her if she could write on any Subject; she said Yes.*

In 1772, Susanna Wheatley collected Phillis' poems and tried to get them published as a book. In February, March, and April, she ran advertisements in the Boston *Censor* for a book of 28 poems. In colonial times, a book was advertised in newspapers to find out if enough people were interested in buying the work. If too few people responded to the ads, then the publisher might choose not to publish it. This saved the expense of printing a book that wouldn't sell well. Susanna Wheatley hoped to find at least 300 people who would agree to buy the teenager's poems.

Few Bostonians responded to the advertisements. In fact, some citizens questioned whether the young slave had written the poems at all. Many people believed that black people were less intelligent than whites. They didn't believe a black teenage slave girl could create such fine poetry.

John Wheatley decided to put an end to the doubts about Phillis. He asked some of the most respectable men in Boston to come together and judge for themselves whether Phillis' poems were her own. Eighteen men, mostly slaveowners, agreed to question Phillis Wheatley and examine her poetry. They included merchants, ministers, politicians, judges, and others. Even the governor and lieutenant governor of the Massachusetts Colony attended. John Hancock was there, too. People would surely believe what this famous leader of the colony had to say about Phillis Wheatley's work.

John Hancock (1737-1793) confirmed that Wheatley wrote her own poetry.

Sometime in the fall of 1772, the men met with Phillis Wheatley. No one wrote down what happened at the meeting, but they probably quizzed her on Greek mythology, the Bible, and other pieces of literature. They may have asked her to write a poem on the spot. Whatever the questions were, Phillis answered them and passed their exam brilliantly. They now believed that Phillis Wheatley was an intelligent person who was capable of writing poetry. The group was impressed and agreed to sign this statement:

> *We whose Names are under-written, do assure the World, that the Poems specified in the following Page, were (as we verily believe) written by Phillis, a young Negro Girl, who was but a few Years since, brought an uncultivated Barbarian from Africa, and has ever since been, and now is, under the Disadvantage of serving as a Slave in a Family in this Town.*

Now there were outstanding witnesses that Phillis Wheatley did have a remarkable gift. It also showed the people of Boston and other cities that they must rethink their ideas about blacks and their abilities. Soon, people who supported freedom and equal rights for blacks would point to Wheatley and ask why blacks were being enslaved if they could accomplish the same things as whites.

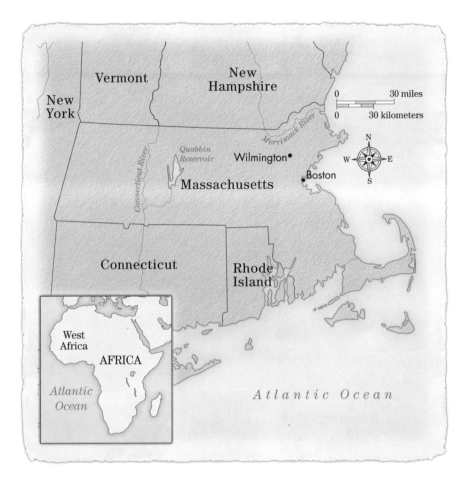

Phillis Wheatley's influence soon went farther than the colonies. She was about to visit England and meet someone who would help publish her first book of poetry. ✎

Phillis Wheatley was born in Africa but lived most of her life in Boston, Massachusetts.

Chapter

5 TRIP TO ENGLAND

❦

Plans were made for Phillis Wheatley to go to England. Her health was not good, and doctors had told the Wheatleys that a sea voyage might help her recover. The Wheatleys decided that Phillis should travel to England with their son, Nathaniel. He recently had taken over his father's business and planned a visit there.

Phillis was excited about her trip. She had been on an ocean voyage before, but her trip from Africa to North America was not something she wanted to remember. As on other important occasions, Wheatley wrote a poem to help her remember her feelings. Although her poem expressed joy at the upcoming trip, it also talked about her sadness at leaving Susanna Wheatley.

She dedicated "A Farewell to America" to her mistress:

> *Susannah mourns, nor can I bear*
> *To see the crystal show'r,*
> *Or mark the tender falling tear*
> *At sad departure's hour.*

There was a second important reason for Wheatley's visit to England: She was going to watch over the printing of her first published book. Despite Phillis' meeting with the 18 respected Bostonians, and even having their letter of recommendation, no publisher in Boston would print her book. Susanna Wheatley wrote to some friends in England who were more willing to help out. One of those friends was Selina Hastings, Countess of Huntingdon. She had become a fan of Wheatley's after reading the elegy she had written about Whitefield, a close friend of hers. She was also an abolitionist, someone eager to put an end to slavery.

Selina Hastings (1707-1791), Countess of Huntingdon, helped Wheatley publish her book.

The countess agreed to help Phillis publish a book. First, however, some of the poems would need to be changed. Patriotic poems, such as "On the Death of Master Seider who was killed by Ebenezer Richardson," were removed completely. The poem talked about an incident in Boston when an 11-year-old boy was killed by a colonist loyal to Britain and involved in spy activities. Poems about the British taking over Boston and the Boston Massacre were also omitted. After all, how could a book published in England include anti-British poetry? Instead, poems that spoke highly of England would be included, such as "To the King's Most Excellent Majesty, 1768." The poem was written for King George III after he repealed the Stamp Act.

On May 8, 1773, Phillis and Nathaniel boarded the Wheatleys' boat, the *London Packet*, and headed to England. The trip took more than a month, but they finally arrived in London on June 17. Phillis Wheatley was greeted

Selina Hastings (1707–1791) was a countess, the wife of the ninth earl of Huntingdon, England. Her sister-in-law, Lady Margaret Hastings, converted her to Methodism, a Protestant religious group. In her newfound faith, Hastings became a strong supporter of the Methodists, building them more than 60 chapels throughout England. She hired ministers and supported leading Methodist preachers like George Whitefield, John Wesley, and Charles Wesley. Her involvement with the Methodists eventually caused her to lose her membership in the state-run Church of England.

warmly and treated as a celebrity. She was invited to social gatherings, where she was asked to read her poetry. She received gifts of books and money.

Many visitors came to the London apartment where Phillis and Nathaniel were staying. One of those visitors was Benjamin Franklin, who had helped convince Britain to repeal the Stamp Act. Franklin often traveled to England to discuss grievances the colonists had against the British. Sometimes, he went to France to ask for help in the colonists' fight for independence. This time, Franklin was making a social call. His nephew had asked him to visit the young slave while she was in London. Wheatley was quite flattered at the Founding Father's visit. However, the meeting didn't go to Franklin's liking, as he reported to his nephew:

> *Upon your recommendation I went to see the black Poetess and offer'd her any Services I could do her. Before I left the house I understood her master was there, and had sent her to me, but did not come into the room himself, and I though was not pleased with the visit. I should perhaps have inquired first for him; but I had heard nothing of him, and I have heard nothing since of her.*

During her six-week stay, Phillis took in some of the sights in London. She was escorted to the Tower of London, where English kings and queens had lived for centuries. Many, too, had been beheaded there for being disloyal to a monarch. Granville Sharp, an English abolitionist, was Phillis' escort. He took her to see the lions, panthers, tigers, and other animals that were kept at the Tower. She also admired the beautiful crowns and jewels of England's royal family that were on display.

Another place she visited was Westminster Abbey, the church that royalty attended and the place where kings and queens were crowned. Then

London, England, in the 18th century; the Thames River on the left and the Tower of London on the right

there was the tour of the British Museum, with its relics from the past, and a trip to the Royal Observatory at Greenwich, a science center. There were many things to be discovered and learned in London. She would later remember her trip to England as the best time of her life. She wrote to Obour about how the British had treated her:

> *The friends I found there among the nobility and gentry, their benevolent conduct towards me, the unexpected and unmerited civility ... with which I was treated by all, fills me with astonishment. I can scarcely realize it.*

Wheatley had also received a great honor—an invitation to meet with the king. She was asked to come to the royal palace in mid-July. King George III was not a popular person in the colonies at that time. When colonists thought of the king, they thought of unfair taxes and the huge British army that invaded Boston. They thought of his government, the British Parliament, which did not allow representatives from America. They remembered the Townshend Acts that put a high tax on glass, paint, paper, and tea. They lived a more difficult life because they were boycotting English goods, refusing to buy anything that was imported from England.

The king represented everything that was unfair

in the colonies. But being granted an audience with King George III was still an honor. It proved that Phillis Wheatley was now a famous poet, not only in the colonies, but in Europe as well. But before Phillis could meet with the king, she received word that Susanna Wheatley was dying. Phillis immediately cancelled her appearance and made plans to return home on the *London Packet* in late July.

Wheatley also never got the chance to meet the

George III was king of England from 1760-1820.

Countess of Huntingdon, who was ill and had left London for her home in Wales. Before Phillis set sail to return to America, she wrote a letter to the countess. Part of it said, "[I am] extremely reluctant to go without having first seen your Ladyship."

But Phillis would not delay her return home to see her ailing mistress. She boarded the ship for the long journey and anxiously awaited the day it would dock in Boston Harbor. The *London Packet* arrived on September 13, 1773, and Phillis hurried to Susanna's bedside. This woman may have been her owner, but she was also her strongest supporter and the closest thing to a mother that Phillis had known throughout most of her life. About six months later, in March 1774, Susanna Wheatley died. Phillis lost her dear friend and companion.

Phillis did not write an elegy for her mistress. But she did write about her deep sorrow in a letter to Obour Tanner:

> *I have lately met with a great trial in the Death of my mistress; let us imagine the loss of a Parent, Sister, or Brother, the tenderness of all these were united in her.—I was a poor little outcast & stranger when she took me in, not only into her house, but I presently became a sharer in her most tender affections. I was treated by her more like a child than her servant.*

Phillis Wheatley's signature at the end of one of the many letters she wrote to her friends

In another letter to Obour, Wheatley wrote that she felt "like one forsaken by her parent in a desolate wilderness. I fear lest every step should lead me into error and confusion."

Susanna Wheatley lived long enough to know that Phillis' book of poems was now in print. In late 1773, *Poems on Various Subjects, Religious and Moral* had been published in England. Susanna had to be pleased to know that her frail little slave was now a famous writer. She had recognized Phillis' intelligence and poetic talent early on. The person she had nurtured and taught was a published author. Now Susanna could share her with the world. ✑

POEMS

ON

VARIOUS SUBJECTS,

RELIGIOUS AND MORAL.

BY

PHILLIS WHEATLEY,

NEGRO SERVANT to Mr. JOHN WHEATLEY,
of BOSTON, in NEW ENGLAND.

—————————————

LONDON:

Printed for A. BELL, Bookseller, Aldgate; and sold by
Meſsrs. COX and BERRY, King-Street, BOSTON.

MDCCLXXIII.

6 THE BOOK

❧❦❧

Poems on Various Subjects, Religious and Moral was dedicated to the Countess of Huntingdon. It was the first book of poetry published by an African-American. In fact, Wheatley was one of the first African-Americans to publish any book at all. Her publisher, Archibald Bell, knew that many people would not believe the book was written by a slave. So he included the statement signed by the men who had questioned Wheatley in Boston. Bell wrote in the preface of the book:

> *The following poems were written originally for the Amusement of the Author, as they were the Products of her leisure Moments. She had no Intention ever to have published them; nor would they now*

The title page of the book of poems by Phillis Wheatley, America's first notable African-American poet have made their Appearance, but at the Importunity of many of her best, and most generous Friends; to whom she considers herself as under the greatest Obligations.

The Countess of Huntingdon thought Phillis' picture should be included in the front of the book. She requested that a sketch be drawn by an artist, although the name of the artist is unknown. It may have been painted by African artist and slave, Scipio Moorhead. Wheatley later composed a poem about Moorhead's paintings.

The likeness of Phillis emphasized who she really was—a slave. She had on clothing commonly worn by a servant, including an apron and a hat. The picture also showed how this woman was a strange combination of slave and writer. In her right hand was a pen, and she was ready to write on a piece of paper. Her face, absorbed in thought, showed what an intelligent person she was. Around the oval frame of the picture were the words, "Phillis Wheatley, Negro Servant to Mr. John Wheatley, of Boston."

John Wheatley also had a part in her book. He wrote a short account of her life, which was placed at the beginning. Who would have known about her life better than John Wheatley?

Bell advertised Phillis' book in London newspapers. He had only the highest praise for his latest writing sensation and her book of poetry. Part of the

advertisement read, "The book ... displays perhaps one of the greatest instances of pure, unassisted genius, that the world ever produced."

A drawing of Phillis Wheatley in her book, Poems on Various Subjects, Religious and Moral

The book sold well throughout London. Copies were sent to other parts of Europe and the American colonies. Wheatley immediately became the most famous black person in Europe and America.

Some of the most influential writers and thinkers of the time read her poetry. One of those people was Voltaire, the famous French author, historian, and philosopher. He commented that Wheatley's work proved that blacks could write poetry.

Voltaire (1694-1778), French writer, read Phillis Wheatley's poetry.

People had many different opinions about her book. Some praised the poet; others praised the poems. Some criticized her and were not particularly impressed with her writing. One person wrote that the poems "display no astonishing power of genius," but they were remarkable because they were written by a black slave. Another person said that her poems had no fire or spirit.

Some people didn't like the book because it was written by a black person. They said she must have just tried to write like someone else. One person couldn't believe Wheatley, a black slave, could create an original poem. Thomas Jefferson was one critic who couldn't see beyond the color of Wheatley's skin. Jefferson, who would one day write the Declaration of Independence and become president of the United States, did not have a high regard for Phillis Wheatley. He wrote, "Religion, indeed has produced a Phillis Whatley [sic]; but it could not produce a

Thomas Jefferson (1743-1826) criticized Phillis Wheatley's writing.

poet. The compositions published under her name are below the dignity of criticism."

Jefferson's comments set off an uproar. Many people leaped to Wheatley's defense. One defender was Samuel Stanhope Smith, the seventh president of the College of New Jersey (later Princeton University). He wrote a response to Jefferson:

Jupiter Hammon was born into slavery in 1711 and owned by the Lloyd family of Long Island, New York. Like Phillis Wheatley, he was an educated slave and wrote poetry. In 1761, the same year Wheatley arrived in Boston, Hammon published his first poem, "An Evening Thought. Salvation by Christ with Penitential Cries: Composed by Jupiter Hammon, a Negro belonging to Mr. Lloyd of Queen's Village, on Long Island, the 25th of December, 1760."

The poems of Phillis Wheatley, a poor African slave, taught to read by the indulgent piety of her master are spoken of with infinite contempt. But I will demand of Mr. Jefferson, or of any other man who is acquainted with American planters, how many of those masters have written poems equal to those of Phillis Wheatley?

For black colonists, Wheatley's accomplishments gave them great inspiration. Another black poet, Jupiter Hammon, wrote a poem in Phillis' honor. It said she was a model for the youth of Boston.

The book was greatly appreciated by Londoners. At least one

English reader could not understand why an intelligent, artistic person like Phillis Wheatley could still be held in slavery. He criticized the freedom-loving colonists in Boston:

> *We are much concerned to find that this ingenious young woman is yet a slave. The people of Boston boast themselves chiefly on their principles of liberty. One such act as the purchase of her freedom would, in our opinion, have done them more honor than hanging a thousand trees with ribbons and emblems.*

Perhaps his words caused some people to think about Phillis' freedom. Perhaps his criticism helped set her free. ✑

7 FREE!

࿇

English critics were quick to write harsh essays about Phillis Wheatley's master. How could he still enslave this famous writer? But they also wondered how Americans could still be enslaving people when they were fighting for their own freedom from Britain. The essays no doubt sped up Phillis' journey to freedom.

It is uncertain exactly when Phillis Wheatley became a free woman. But in October 1773, she wrote about her new freedom to a friend, David Wooster. "Since my return to America my Master, has at the desire of my friends in England given me my freedom." She knew the people of England had pressured John Wheatley to grant her freedom, and for that she was grateful.

Phillis Wheatley was granted her freedom around 1773.

Now at about the age of 20, Phillis Wheatley was free. John Wheatley signed a deed of manumission, an official document giving Phillis her freedom. She was now free to write openly about what she thought of slavery. Her letter to Samson Occom compared American slaves to Egyptian slaves of ancient times. The letter was published in many area newspapers in 1774. Part of it said:

In every human Breast, God has implanted a Principle, which we call Love of Freedom; it is impatient of Oppression, and pants for Deliverance; and by the Leave of our modern Egyptians I will assert, that the same Principle lives in us.

Phillis Wheatley was given her individual freedom in about 1773, but it was almost 90 years later before slavery began to be officially banned in the United States. Emancipation, the freeing of slaves, began on January 1, 1863, when President Abraham Lincoln issued the Emancipation Proclamation. It declared that all persons held as slaves in Southern states were now free.

The letter also proclaimed how odd it was that colonists were crying out for America's freedom, and at the same time they were enslaving a whole race of people. She described it as the "strange Absurdity of their Conduct whose Words and actions are so diametrically [completely] opposite." The letter was one of the first antislavery letters written by

A slave is handed a deed of manumussion, a document granting her freedom.

a black person in America.

With freedom came responsibility for Phillis Wheatley. For the first time, she was in charge of her future. She needed to find a way to survive as a free black woman in Boston. John Wheatley said she could still live at the Wheatley mansion, and Phillis was grateful for his kindness. She wrote to a friend, "I hope ever to retain a grateful sense, and treat him with that respect which is ever due a paternal friendship."

In an attempt to support herself, Phillis turned to her book. She was paid half the price of each book. If she could sell more books, she could make enough money to survive.

I am to have half the Sale of the Books. I am now upon my own footing and what- ever I get by this is entirely min, & it is the Chief I have to depend upon.

She ordered a shipment of her books from England, and 300 copies arrived in Boston in early 1774. She worked hard to sell them, writing to friends and acquaintances and asking others in per- son if they would buy her book. Obour Tanner also asked people to buy the book and was able to sell six copies. Samson Occom sold some, too.

But book sales were not going very well. Perhaps the timing was not right. The people of Boston were probably more concerned with the unrest in the colonies, especially in Boston.

The year 1774 started off brightly for Phillis but quickly turned dismal. In the spring, Britain sent more troops to occupy Boston. A British military officer arrived to act as governor and take charge of Massachusetts. The British closed down Boston Harbor, and no colonial ships were allowed to enter or leave. Bostonians were forced to allow British soldiers to live in their homes. They even had to feed them. The Wheatley house had an unwanted British

British soldiers occupy the city of Boston, Massachusetts.

resident—Lieutenant Rochfort. Phillis' poem titled "A Gentleman of the Navy" was probably directed at this unwelcome soldier.

In September, representatives from every colony except Georgia met in Philadelphia. The colonists called it the Continental Congress. Members agreed to stop all trade with Britain. They also said colonists no longer had to obey British laws that took away their freedoms as citizens.

On April 19, 1775, hostilities exploded between Britain and the colonists. Seven hundred British soldiers arrived at Boston Harbor and marched to Lexington, Massachusetts. They were on their way to Concord, Massachusetts, to search Colonel James Barrett's farm for weapons. At Lexington, 77 colonial soldiers were waiting for them, and shots were fired. British troops continued to Concord, where more than 300 minutemen were ready to fight. On their way back, rebel soldiers attacked the British, and the battle spread. Soldiers on both sides were killed, but the worn-out British retreated and returned to their ships in Boston harbor. The Revolutionary War had begun.

John Wheatley's daughter, Mary, and her husband, John Lathrop, left Boston for a safer city— Providence, Rhode Island. Five months later, John Wheatley joined them there. No one knows if Phillis went with Wheatley or stayed in Boston.

At first, Phillis hoped for a peaceful end to the problems between Britain and America. She was fond of England and its kind people, but now she eagerly supported the colonies. She wanted them to be free of Britain's rule. As she had done before, she started putting her feelings into poetry. Those feelings were passionate for the colonial cause.

The Battle of Lexington on April 19, 1775, sparked the beginning of the Revolutionary War.

8 POET OF THE REVOLUTION

⨏⨕⨐

Members of the Continental Congress met again in May 1775 to discuss what to do now that battles had broken out. They decided the colonies needed an army, and George Washington of Virginia was chosen to head up the new Continental Army.

Washington left Philadelphia and headed for Boston. News spread quickly throughout the colonies about Washington and his Army of about 14,500 colonial soldiers who had no training and no official uniforms.

Phillis Wheatley was inspired by these events and wrote a poem in Washington's honor. She sent it to him with a letter that described how happy she was at his new position. With modesty, she asked the general to forgive any mistakes she

George Washington takes command of the Continental Army in May 1775.

might have made. Wheatley ended the letter, "Wishing your Excellency all possible success in the great cause you are so generously engaged in." Perhaps the poem would inspire this great leader to victory:

> *Proceed, great chief, with virtue on thy side,*
> *Thy ev'ry action let the goddess guide.*
> *A crown, a mansion, and a throne that shine,*
> *With gold unfading, WASHINGTON! be thine.*

Washington's success would mean freedom for the colonies, something Wheatley wanted very much. She believed freedom was established by God and that Washington would triumph. Her beloved "Columbia," her poetic name for America, was suffering, and she asked an angelic choir to take notice:

> *Celestial choir! enthron'd in realms of light,*
> *Columbia's scenes of glorious toils I write.*
> *While freedom's cause her anxious breast alarms,*
> *She flashes dreadful in refulgent [splendid] arms.*
> *See mother earth her offspring's fate bemoan,*
> *And nations gaze at scenes before unknown!*

Her patriotic poetry won her the admiration of many colonists. In February 1776, Phillis Wheatley received a letter from Washington, who was at Army headquarters in Cambridge,

Massachusetts. In the midst of a raging war and a difficult winter, the general took time to answer her letter and praise her poetry. He thanked her

A reproduction of George Washington's letter to Phillis Wheatley

Cambridge February 28th 1776.

Mrs Phillis,

Your favour of the 26. of October did not reach my hands till the middle of December. Time enough, you will say, to have given an answer ere this. Granted. But a variety of important occurrences, continually interposing to distract the mind and withdraw the attention, I hope will apologize for the delay, and plead my excuse for the seeming, but not real, neglect.

I thank you most sincerely for your polite notice of me, in the elegant Lines you enclosed; and however undeserving I may be of such encomium and panegyrick, the style and manner exhibit a striking proof of your great poetical Talents. In honour of which, and as a tribute justly due to you, I would have published the Poem, had I not been apprehensive, that, while I only meant to give the World this new instance of your genius, I might have incurred the imputation of Vanity. This, and nothing else, determined me not to give it place in the public Prints.

If you should ever come to Cambridge, or near Head Quarters, I shall be happy to see a person so favoured by the Muses, and to whom Nature has been so liberal and beneficent in her dispensations.

I am, with great Respect,
Your obedt humble servant,

for the poem and apologized for not responding sooner. Part of his warm, flattering letter said:

> [A]s a tribute justly due to you, I would have published the poem, had I not been apprehensive, that, while I only meant to give the world this new instance of your genius, I might have incurred the imputation of vanity. ... If you should ever come to Cambridge, or near headquarters, I shall be happy to see a person so favored by the Muses.

During and after the Revolutionary War, Phillis Wheatley and other poets often used the name Columbia in their poetry to stand for America. Columbia is the female form of Columbus, taken from the explorer Christopher Columbus. The capital of the United States came to be called Washington, after the first president, George Washington. It was also named the District of Columbia.

Phillis accepted the general's offer to visit him at headquarters. She met with him in Cambridge for about half an hour. Within about a month, Washington had Wheatley's poem published.

Soon after, Washington's Army successfully forced the British army out of Boston. Many Bostonians could now return to their homes. The city was not the same as they had left it, however. It was no longer a vibrant colonial center. British soldiers had chopped down most of the trees for firewood. Even wooden buildings were pulled apart and burned to keep the British troops warm. One of those buildings was the Old North Church, where John Lathrop was the minister. Less than a year before, two lanterns had hung in the steeple of that church to warn a patriot named Paul Revere that

Two lanterns in the belfry of the Old North Church signaled the British had come by sea.

British troops were coming by sea. The Wheatley home was severely damaged, too, when it was accidentally hit by colonial cannons.

In December 1776, the Wheatley family returned to Boston. Although it was a happy time to be back in their home city, it was also the beginning of hardships and sadness for Phillis. In 1778, John Wheatley died. That same year, Phillis' beloved tutor and friend, Mary Lathrop, also died. Mary's brother Nathaniel had died five years before while living in England.

Now all the Wheatleys were gone. John Wheatley left a will, but he didn't leave any part of his money or possessions to his former slave. For this woman in her mid-20s, the future looked bleak. There were not many jobs available in Boston at that time, especially for a black woman whose main skill was writing poetry. Many artists found it difficult to get a job.

Free blacks had to compete with white people for jobs. Sometimes, free blacks even competed with black slaves whose masters hired them out to make more money for themselves. Slavery was becoming less accepted in Massachusetts, but people still preferred to hire white people to fill the jobs. Wheatley began experiencing the hardships of discrimination that free blacks in other colonies were suffering.

Phillis had many friends in England, but how could she ask for their help when the colonies were at war with Britain? She also had friends and supporters in Massachusetts and some of the other colonies, but they were concerned for their families and their country. They really didn't have time for Phillis. But one friend she had known for five years did have time for her. In fact, he eventually asked her to marry him.

John Peters ran a grocery store on Court Street in Boston. Some said he also worked as a baker, a physician, and even a lawyer, arguing cases for other blacks in the city from time to time. This very handsome free black man with his distinguished wig and cane looked like an extraordinary gentleman.

Phillis Wheatley's husband, John Peters, had several businesses in downtown Boston, Massachusetts.

With his proper manners and very courteous

conduct, he persuaded Phillis to marry him in April 1778. Soon after their marriage, Peters' business failed. He tried his hand at other businesses, but they also failed. After a while, he stopped trying new ventures, and his attempts to find other work in Boston were unsuccessful.

Many thought Peters was a smart man. One person called him "a remarkable specimen of his race, being a fluent writer, a ready speaker." The Wheatleys' granddaughter later remembered that Peters was not only a remarkable looking man, but he was also respectable and intelligent. Others said he was irresponsible and proud. Some said he just put on the airs of a gentleman. Obour was not happy that Phillis had married Peters and even said, "[P]oor Phillis let herself down by marrying."

Since Peters didn't have a job, Phillis tried to find a way to make money. At first, she hoped to make ends meet by writing more poetry. In 1779, she attempted to get a second book of poetry published.

She ran six advertisements in local newspapers in hopes of finding enough interest to publish her book. Her ads described a 300-page volume, dedicated to "Right Hon. Benjamin Franklin, Esq: One of the Ambassadors of the United States at the Court of France." The book would have 33 poems and 13 letters. Few people responded to her advertisements, however, and she was forced to abandon the idea.

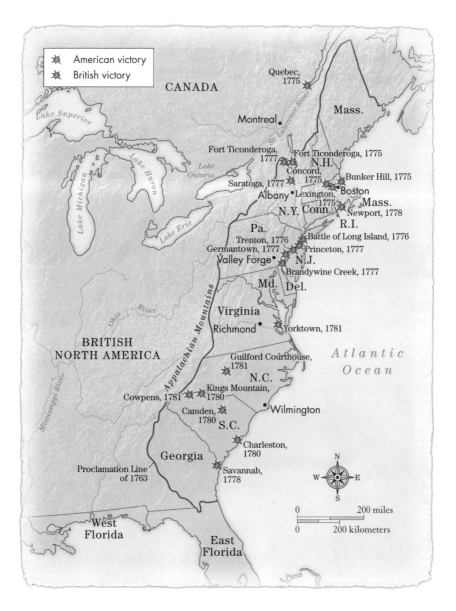

As the war raged and spread in 1779, the colonists were optimistic that freedom was possible. In spite of the difficult winter, the Continental

Major battles of the American Revolution were fought throughout the colonies.

Army had endured at Valley Forge, Pennsylvania, in 1777-1778, the colonists still believed the British could be defeated.

In May 1778, France had agreed to join the Americans in their fight for independence, and more optimism spread. Fighting increased with the arrival of the French army, and living in large cities like Boston became more dangerous. For their safety, many citizens left the cities and went to smaller country towns. Phillis and her husband left Boston in 1779 and moved to Wilmington, Massachusetts, where they lived for several years. They started a family while they were there, having three children in three years. But unfortunately, the couple's first two children died as babies. Life was full of sorrows and hardships for Phillis.

No one was sure about the events of Phillis' life while she was in Wilmington. She hadn't communicated with her friends for quite some time, but she did know where Obour was. On May 16, 1779, Phillis wrote to her in Worcester, Massachusetts:

> *By this opportunity I have the pleasure to inform you that I am well and hope you are so; tho' I have been silent, I have not been unmindful of you, but a variety of hindrances was the cause of my not writing to you. But in time to come I hope our correspondence will revive—and revive*

*in better times—pray write me soon, for I
long to hear from you—you may depend
on constant replies.*

No one knows if Obour ever answered the letter or if the two ever saw each other again. Phillis' circumstances may have prevented her from continuing the friendship.

After spending three years in Wilmington, Phillis moved back to Boston. She came back without her husband and lived for six weeks with one of the Wheatleys' nieces in a run-down house. Some say Peters abandoned her and disappeared for a while. Others said he was in a Massachusetts debtor's prison for failure to pay his debts. In any case, Phillis had to support herself and her little child.

Phillis took a job as a scrub maid at a boardinghouse. Even though she had grown up as a slave, she had not had to do hard physical labor like she was doing now. She still had health problems that had plagued her all her life. She soon discovered that she wasn't strong enough for the job and became even more ill.

John Peters eventually reunited with his wife in Boston, and they moved into a run-down apartment. Phillis still bore the responsibility of supporting the family. She needed help, but she found none. Those people who had admired her and fussed over her when she was the Wheatleys' slave were not there for her now. She probably didn't expect much from them, but she did hope her old admirers would do something. She shared her feelings in a letter to a friend, John Thornton:

> *The world is a severe Schoolmaster, for its frowns are less dang'rous than its Smiles and flatteries, and it is a difficult task to keep in the path of Wisdom. I ... find exactly true your thoughts on the behavior of those who seem'd to respect me while under my mistress's patronage: you said right, for Some of those have already put on a reserve.*

The final years of Wheatley's life were spent in poverty and loneliness. After her marriage and with the burden of supporting herself and her family, Phillis wrote less and less poetry. People lost contact with this intelligent, artistic woman, and no one knew much about the last part of her life.

Her health declined rapidly, and on December 5, 1784, the 31-year-old African-American poet died at a boardinghouse. She was penniless, practically unknown, and alone, except for her sick little toddler. Very soon after her death, her child also died. Mother and child were buried together in the same unmarked grave. They were probably buried in Boston, but no one knows where that anonymous grave is located.

Before Wheatley died, she experienced the end of the Revolutionary War and a colonial victory. She probably knew about the 1781 British surrender at Yorktown, Virginia, and she no doubt heard about the British troops going back to England. In 1784, she wrote one of her last poems, "Liberty and

The British surrender at Yorktown on October 19, 1781.

Peace," about the defeat of Britain (Britannia). Part of it reads:

> *E'en great Britannia sees with dread Surprize,*
> *And from the dazzl'ing Splendor turns her eyes!*

Britain was surprised by a colonial victory, and Phillis was delighted that the United States of America was now shining in dazzling splendor. England was one of her favorite places, and the people had been good to her, but she valued her country's freedom more.

The America she loved had given her great praise during her lifetime. She, in turn, had enthusiastically written poetry about her country, "Columbia," and she considered it a privilege to live in America. It was also her privilege to have met the celebrated General Washington and to have honored him in her poetry.

On April 30, 1789, George Washington was inaugurated as the first presi-

Phillis Wheatley (1753?-1784)

George Washington is inaugurated as the first president of the United States on April 30, 1789.

dent of the United States of America. If Phillis Wheatley had lived longer, she undoubtedly would have celebrated the event. She probably would have taken her pen and paper and hailed Washington in poetry as the new leader of her country.

Wheatley greatly valued her country's independence, and she rejoiced in each of its victories. She also valued her own personal freedom and freedom for all African-Americans. How sad that this woman who loved freedom so much suffered and lived in poverty as a free person. ❧

PHILLIS WHEATLEY

CA. 1753-1784

BORN IN WEST AFRICA AND SOLD AS A SLAVE
FROM THE SHIP *PHILLIS* IN COLONIAL BOSTON,
SHE WAS A LITERARY PRODIGY WHOSE 1773 VOLUME
*POEMS ON VARIOUS SUBJECTS, RELIGIOUS,
AND MORAL* WAS THE FIRST BOOK PUBLISHED BY
AN AFRICAN WRITER IN AMERICA.

9

Chapter

A PLACE IN HISTORY

❦

News of Phillis Wheatley's death was printed in several newspapers throughout Massachusetts and the surrounding colonies. The articles celebrated her life, her accomplishments, and her poetry. They seldom mentioned that she was a former slave or that she had died in poverty and was buried in an unknown grave.

Throughout her life, Wheatley expressed sorrow over many people who had died and wrote elegies in their honor. Now someone honored Wheatley in the same way. A poet who merely called himself Horace published a 54-line elegy for her. It was called "Elegy on the Death of a Late Celebrated Poetess."

Horace must have known about Phillis' hardships during her later years. He also must have

Bronze statue of Phillis Wheatley is part of a display at the Boston Women's Memorial.

known about her strong belief in an eternal life. The elegy ends:

> Tho' now the business of her life is o'er,
> Tho' now she breathes and tunes her lyre no more;
> Tho' now the body mixes with the clay;
> The soul wings upward to immortal day;
> Free'd from a world of wo, and scene of cares,
> A lyre of gold she tunes, a crow of glory wears.

Wheatley's husband sold many of her books and unpublished poems after she died. Yet for at least 50 years after her death, Wheatley's book of poetry went mostly unnoticed. In the 1830s, however, her poems again became popular among abolitionists.

Her intelligence helped them disprove arguments that blacks were not as smart as whites. They pointed to this slave poet as an example of what blacks might accomplish, if given the opportunity. Wheatley also served as an important model for those who wanted to end slavery.

Almost 34 years after Wheatley's death, another slave, Frederick Douglass, emerged to join her as an example of success. Douglass, an escaped slave, started an antislavery newspaper in 1847. Many of Wheatley's poems had been published in another antislavery newspaper, *The Liberator*, and perhaps Douglass read her poetry there.

In 1834, some of Wheatley's poems were pub-

lished in *Memoir and Poems of Phillis Wheatley.* Thirty years later, *Letters of Phillis Wheatley, the Negro Slave-Poet of Boston*, was published. At a time when slavery was dividing the country, Wheatley's poetry gave encouragement to people who were fighting against it.

But several years after slavery came to an end in

Phillis Wheatley's poetry appeared in The Liberator, a *newspaper published by William Lloyd Garrison, abolitionist of the mid-1800s.*

More than 60 years after Phillis Wheatley died, Frederick Douglass (1818–1895) wrote about what it was like to be a slave. In 1845, he published his life story, Narrative of the Life of Frederick Douglass, an American Slave. In the book, he told about his life as a slave under cruel masters. In the first four months, about 5,000 copies were sold in the United States and Europe. This autobiography helped the fight against slavery in the United States.

the United States, people's opinions about Wheatley began to change. Many black critics began to condemn her for not speaking out more strongly against slavery. In the 1920s, people criticized her for not being angry about being taken out of Africa and shipped to America to become a slave.

One writer and poet, James Weldon Johnson, wrote about Wheatley's poetry, "One looks in vain for some outburst or even complaint against the bondage of her people." He believed her poems showed a "smug contentment at her escape" from Africa.

Others said that Wheatley was celebrated not for the value of her poetry. They claimed that her fame was because she was a black woman writing at a time when most blacks in America were enslaved and illiterate.

In the 1960s, black leaders spoke out strongly against her. During this time of great racial unrest, many blacks were anti-Wheatley. They thought she accepted the way that whites viewed blacks and that she had a "white mind."

James Weldon Johnson, American poet, wrote a memorial poem called "Fifty Years" in 1913 on the 50th anniversary of the Emancipation Proclamation.

Lately, people have started to take another look at Wheatley's poetry. Some say her poems shouldn't be judged on whether they are black or white. They should remind the world that there are no black minds or white minds—just minds.

Wheatley's poems provide a glimpse into the heart of a person who cared deeply for people and for her country. They tell about the interesting times in which she lived and provide a glimpse of the

On being brought from AFRICA to AMERICA.

'TWAS mercy brought me from my *Pagan* land,
Taught my benighted foul to understand
That there's a God, that there's a *Saviour* too;
Once I redemption neither fought nor knew.
Some view our fable race with fcornful eye,
"Their colour is a diabolic die."
Remember, *Chriftians, Negros*, black as *Cain*,
May be refin'd, and join th' angelic train.

VARIOUS SUBJECTS.

On the Death of the Rev. Dr. SEWELL. 1769.

ERE yet the morn its lovely bluthes fpread,
See Sewell number'd with the happy dead.
Hail, holy man, arriv'd th' immortal fhore,
Though we fhall hear thy warning voice no more.
Come, let us all behold with wifhful eyes
The faint afcending to his native fkies;
From hence the prophet wing'd his rapt'rous way
To the bleft manfions in eternal day.
Then begging for the Spirit of our God,
And panting eager for the fame abode,
Come, let us all with the fame vigour rife,
And take a profpect of the blifsful fkies;
While on our minds *Chrift's* image is imprefs,
And the dear Saviour glows in ev'ry breaft.
Thrice happy faint! to find thy heav'n at laft,
What compenfation for the evils paft!

POEMS
ON
VARIOUS SUBJECTS,
RELIGIOUS AND MORAL.
BY
PHILLIS WHEATLEY,
NEGRO SERVANT to Mr. JOHN WHEATLEY,
of BOSTON, in NEW ENGLAND.

LONDON:
Printed for A. BELL, Bookfeller, Aldgate; and fold by
Meffrs. COX and BERRY, King-Street, BOSTON.
MDCCLXXIII.

Copies of Wheatley's book are displayed at the Old South Church, Boston, Massachusetts.

Revolutionary War era.

In a time when most people didn't think slavery was wrong, Phillis Wheatley shared her feelings from a slave's point of view. She was an exceptional person with a brilliant mind, and she had a kind master who allowed her to learn and develop her extraordinary poetic talent.

Wheatley made her mark on history as the author of the first book of poetry by an African-American. In her short life, she wrote nearly 150 poems about religion, slavery, America, freedom, and death.

Her accomplishments earned her a significant place in history. She is an important symbol of what people can do when given the opportunity. ✍

WHEATLEY'S LIFE

1753 OR 1754

Born in Africa

1761

Kidnapped in Africa
and taken to Boston,
Massachusetts; sold
as a slave to
John Wheatley

1765

Writes first known
letter to the
Reverend Samson
Occom

1760

1759

The British
Museum opens
in London

1762

Catherine the Great
becomes empress of
Russia and rules for
34 years

WORLD EVENTS

1767

First published
poem is printed in
the *Newport
Mercury,* a Rhode
Island newspaper

1770

Writes poem
about the
Boston Massacre

1771

Baptized at
the Old South
Church in Boston

1770

1768

British explorer
James Cook
leaves England
for a three-year
exploration of
the Pacific Ocean

1770

Clergyman and chemist
Joseph Priestly gives
rubber its name when he
discovers it rubs out
pencil marks

WHEATLEY'S LIFE

1773

Travels to England;
*Poems on Various
Subjects, Religious
and Moral* is
published; is granted
her freedom

1772

Interviewed by
18 respected
Bostonians to
determine if she
is capable of
writing poetry

P O E M S

ON

VARIOUS SUBJECTS,

RELIGIOUS AND MORAL.

BY

PHILLIS WHEATLEY,

NEGRO SERVANT to Mr. JOHN WHEATLEY,
of BOSTON, in NEW ENGLAND.

L O N D O N:
Printed for A. BELL, Bookseller, Aldgate; and sold by
Messrs. COX and BERRY, King-street, BOSTON.

M DCC LXXIII.

1774

Owner Susanna
Wheatley dies

1774

King Louis XV
of France dies
and his grandson,
Louis XVI
is crowned

1772

Poland is partitioned for
the first time between
Prussia and Austria

WORLD EVENTS

1776

Receives letter from George Washington and visits him in Cambridge, Massachusetts

1775

Writes a poem in honor of George Washington

1775

1775

English novelist Jane Austen born

1776

Scottish economist Adam Smith publishes *The Wealth of Nations*, heralding the beginning of modern economics

WHEATLEY'S LIFE

1778

Marries John Peters; owner John Wheatley dies; teacher Mary Lathrop dies

1779

Efforts to publish a second book of poetry fail; moves to Wilmington, Massachusetts

1779-82

Has three children

1780

1779

Jan Ingenhousz of the Netherlands discovers that plants release oxygen when exposed to sunlight

1778

French writer Voltaire dies

WORLD EVENTS

1782

Moves back to
Boston; works
as a maid

1784

Dies alone and
penniless in Boston
boardinghouse on
December 5

1785

1783

The first manned
hot air balloon
flight is made in
Paris, France, by the
Montgolfier brothers

1786

The British
government
announces its
plan to make
Australia a
penal colony

DATE OF BIRTH: 1753 or 1754

BIRTHPLACE: Probably modern-day
Senegal or Gambia,
West Africa

FATHER: Unknown

MOTHER: Unknown

EDUCATION: No formal education

SPOUSE: John Peters

DATE OF
MARRIAGE: April 1778

CHILDREN: Three (names unknown);
two died as infants,
one as a toddler

DATE OF DEATH: December 5, 1784

PLACE OF BURIAL: Unknown

IN THE LIBRARY

Bloom, Harold, ed. *African-American Poets:
Phillis Wheatley Through Melvin B. Tolson.*
Philadelphia, Pa.: Chelsea House Publishers, 2003.

Gregson, Susan R. *Phillis Wheatley.* Mankato,
Minn.: Capstone Press, 2002.

Redmond, Shirley-Ray. *Patriots in Petticoats:
Heroines of the American Revolution.* New York:
Random House, 2004.

Salisbury, Cynthia. *Phillis Wheatley: Legendary
African-American Poet.* Berkeley Heights, N.J.:
Enslow Publishers, 2001.

Williams, Jean Kinney. *African-Americans in the
Colonies.* Minneapolis: Compass Point Books, 2002.

LOOK FOR MORE SIGNATURE LIVES
BOOKS ABOUT THIS ERA:

Abigail Adams: *Courageous Patriot and First Lady*

Samuel Adams: *Patriot and Statesman*

Ethan Allen: *Green Mountain Rebel*

Benedict Arnold: *From Patriot to Traitor*

Benjamin Franklin: *Scientist and Statesman*

Alexander Hamilton: *Founding Father and Statesman*

John Hancock: *Signer for Independence*

John Paul Jones: *Father of the American Navy*

Thomas Paine: *Great Writer of the Revolution*

Mercy Otis Warren: *Author and Historian*

Martha Washington: *First Lady of the United States*

On the Web

For more information on *Phillis Wheatley*, use FactHound to track
down Web sites related to this book.

1. Go to *www.facthound.com*
2. Type in a search word related to this book or this book ID: 075650984X
3. Click on the *Fetch It* button.

FactHound will find the best
Web sites for you.

Historic Sites

Old South Meeting House
310 Washington St.
Boston, MA 02108
617/482-6439
To visit the church that
Phillis Wheatley attended

Boston National Historical Park
Charlestown Navy Yard
Boston, MA 02129
617/242-5642
To take a walking tour of the
historical sites in the city of Boston

abolitionist
someone who supported the banning of slavery

auction block
a sale where people bid on things (or people, during times of slavery)

deed of manumission
an official document granting freedom to a slave

discrimination
unfair treatment of a person or group, usually because of race

dysentery
disease of the intestines marked by severe diarrhea

elegy
a poem expressing sorrow for one who is dead

minutemen
a group of men ready to take up arms at a minute's notice during the American Revolution

muses
goddesses in Greek mythology that preside over song, poetry, arts, and science

Parliament
part of the British government that makes laws

regiment
a military group made up of about 1,000 soldiers

repeal
to officially cancel something, such as a law

secede
to withdraw from

smallpox
a contagious disease marked by skin eruptions

Chapter 1

Page 12, line 6: Henry Louis Gates Jr. *The Trials of Phillis Wheatley*. New York: Basic Civitas Books, 2003, p. 16.

Page 12, line 12: William H. Robinson. *Phillis Wheatley and Her Writings*. New York: Garland Publishing, Inc., 1984, p. 5.

Chapter 2

Page 16, line 2: *The Trials of Phillis Wheatley*, p. 17.

Page 17, line 13: M.A. Richmond. *Bid the Vassal Soar*. Washington, D.C.: Howard University Press, 1974, p. 13.

Chapter 3

Page 22, line 7: *The Trials of Phillis Wheatley*, p. 19.

Page 27, line 8: *Phillis Wheatley and Her Writings*, p. 24.

Page 28, line 15: Ibid., p. 129.

Page 29, line 3: Ibid., p. 23.

Page 30, line 10: "To the Right Honourable William, Earl of Dartmouth." *Africans in America*. http://www.pbs.org/wgbh/aia/part2/2h20t.html.

Chapter 4

Page 34, line 9: *The Trials of Phillis Wheatley*, p. 70.

Page 38, line 8: "The Case of a Slave Poet, A Forgotten Historical Episode." *U.S. Department of State, International Information Programs*. http://usinfo.state.gov/usa/blackhis/s032602.htm.

Page 39, line 9: Phillis Wheatley. *Poems on Various Subjects, Religious and Moral*. London: 1773. http://darkwing.uoregon.edu/~rbear/wheatley.html.

Page 42, line 3: *Phillis Wheatley and Her Writings*, p. 23.

Page 44, line 12: Ibid., p. 28.

Chapter 5

Page 48, line 3: Phillis Wheatley. *The Collected Works of Phillis Wheatley*. New York: Oxford University Press, 1988, p. 120.

Page 50, line 17: *Phillis Wheatley and Her Writings*, p. 36.

Page 54, line 4: Kenny J. Williams. "Phillis Wheatley." *Dictionary of Literary Biography, Volume 50: Afro-American Writers Before the Harlem Renaissance*. Detroit, Mich.: Gale Research Company, 2003, pp. 245-259.

Page 54, line 20: *Phillis Wheatley and Her Writings*, p. 37.

Page 55, line 2: Ibid., p. 45.

Chapter 6

Page 57, line 11: *The Collected Works of Phillis Wheatley*, preface.

Page 59, line 1: *The Trials of Phillis Wheatley*, p. 32.

Page 61, line 5: "Phillis Wheatley (Peters)." *DISCovering Authors*. Detroit, Mich.: Gale, 2003.

Page 61, line 27: *The Trials of Phillis Wheatley*, pp. 42-44.

Page 62, line 8: *Bid the Vassal Soar*, p. 53.

Page 63, line 5: *Phillis Wheatley and Her Writings*, p. 39.

Chapter 7

Page 65, line 11: *Phillis Wheatley and Her Writings*, p. 40.

Page 66, line 9: *The Trials of Phillis Wheatley*, p. 73.

Page 67, line 8: "Letter to Reverend Samson Occum, 1774." *Africans in America.* http://www.pbs.org/wgvh/aia/part2/2h19.html

Page 68, line 7: *Phillis Wheatley and Her Writings*, p. 40.

Chapter 8

Page 74, line 2: *The Trials of Phillis Wheatley*, p. 39.

Page 74, line 6: "To His Excellency General Washington." *Exploring Poetry.* Detroit, Mich.: Gale, 1997. http://www.galegroup.com/free_resources/ poets/poems/genwashington.htm.

Page 74, line 17: *The Trials of Phillis Wheatley*, p. 38.

Page 76, line 3: *Phillis Wheatley and Her Writings*, p. 53.

Page 82, line 22: Katherine Clay Bassard. *Spiritual Interrogations: Culture, Gender, and Community in Early African American Women's Writing.* Princeton, N.J.: Princeton University Press, 1999, p. 24.

Page 84, line 5: Vincent Carretta and Philip Gould (Eds.). *Genius in Bondage: Literature of the Early Black Atlantic.* Lexington, Ky.: University Press of Kentucky, 2001, p. 182.

Page 86, line 2: Phillis Wheatley. "Liberty and Peace." http://www.4literature.net/Phillis_Wheatley/Liberty_and_Peace/

Chapter 9

Page 90, line 2: *Phillis Wheatley and Her Writings*, p. 64.

Page 92, line 12: *The Trials of Phillis Wheatley*, p. 75.

Bassard, Katherine Clay. *Spiritual Interrogations: Culture, Gender, and Community in Early African American Women's Writing*. Princeton, N.J.: Princeton University Press, 1999.

Carretta, Vincent, and Philip Gould, eds. *Genius in Bondage: Literature of the Early Black Atlantic*. Lexington, Ky.: University Press of Kentucky, 2001.

"The Case of a Slave Poet, A Forgotten Historical Episode." *U.S. Department of State, International Information Programs*. http://usinfo.state.gov/usa/blackhis/s032602.htm.

Gates Jr., Henry Louis. *The Trials of Phillis Wheatley*. New York: Basic Civitas Books, 2003.

"Phillis Wheatley (Peters)." *DISCovering Authors*. Detroit, Mich.: Gale, 2003.

Richmond, M.A. *Bid the Vassal Soar*. Washington, D.C.: Howard University Press, 1974.

Robinson, William H. *Phillis Wheatley and Her Writings*. New York: Garland Publishing, Inc., 1984.

"To His Excellency General Washington." *Exploring Poetry*. Detroit, Mich.: Gale, 1997. http://www.gale.com/free_resources/poets/poems/genwashington.htm.

"To the Right Honourable William, Earl of Dartmouth." *Africans in America*. http://www.pbs.org/wgbh/aia/part2/2h20t.html.

Wheatley, Phillis. *The Collected Works of Phillis Wheatley*. New York: Oxford University Press, 1988.

Wheatley, Phillis. "Letter to Reverend Samson Occum, 1774." *Africans in America*. http://www.pbs.org/wgvh/aia/part2/2h19.html.

Wheatley, Phillis. "Liberty and Peace." http://www.4literature.net/Phillis_Wheatley/Liberty_and_Peace/

Wheatley, Phillis. *Poems on Various Subjects, Religious and Moral*. http://darkwing.uoregon.edu/~rbear/wheatley.html.

Williams, Kenny J. "Phillis Wheatley." *Dictionary of Literary Biography, Volume 50: Afro-American Writers Before the Harlem Renaissance*. Detroit, Mich.: Gale Research Company, 2003.

Robin S. Doak has been writing for children for more than 16 years. A former editor of *Weekly Reader* and *U*S*Kids* magazine, Doak has authored fun and educational materials for kids of all ages. She is a past winner of the Educational Press Association of America Distinguished Achievement Award. She lives with her husband and three children in central Connecticut.

Image Credits